Quiz: 36184
EN

$15.00

Attack and Defense

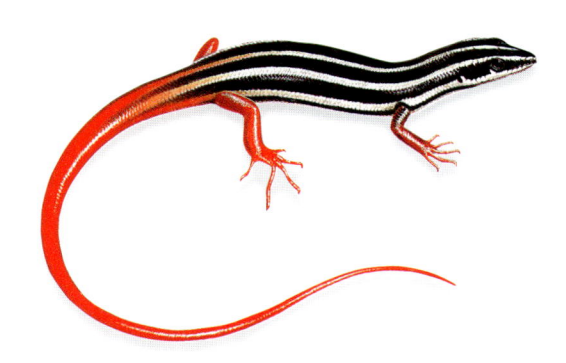

Murphy School
Woodridge School Dist. 68
Woodridge, IL 60517

43733

Text: Robert Coupe
Consultant: George McKay, Conservation Biologist

This edition first published 2003 by
MASON CREST PUBLISHERS INC.
370 Reed Road
Broomall, PA 19008

All rights reserved. No part of this publication may be reproduced or transmitted in any form or by any means, electronic or mechanical, including photocopying, recording, taping, or any information storage and retrieval system, without permission in writing from the publisher.

© Weldon Owen Inc.
Conceived and produced by
Weldon Owen Pty Limited

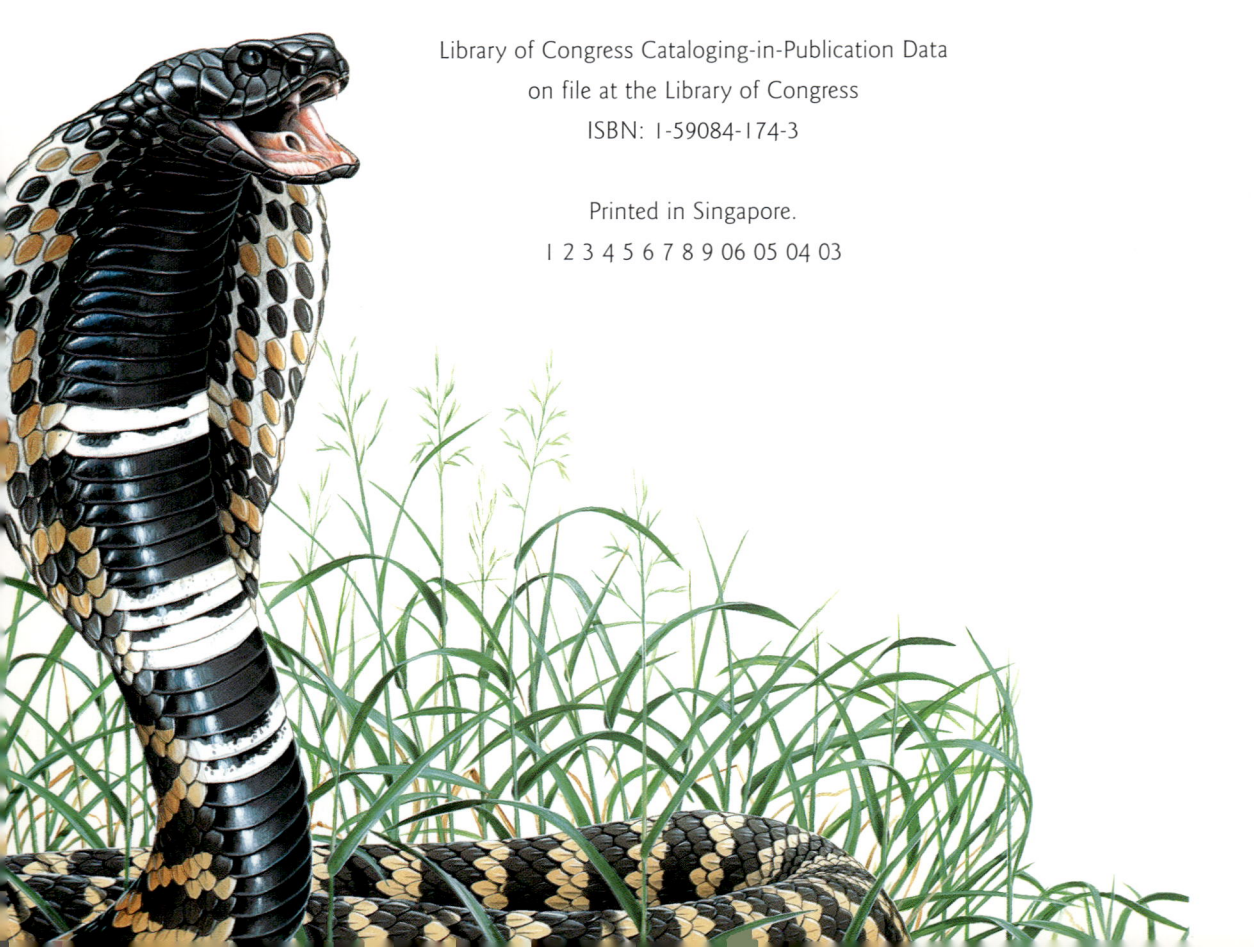

Library of Congress Cataloging-in-Publication Data
on file at the Library of Congress
ISBN: 1-59084-174-3

Printed in Singapore.
1 2 3 4 5 6 7 8 9 06 05 04 03

Contents

The Big Cats	4
Fanged Creatures	6
Bears	8
Sharks	10
Scaly Hunters	12
Whales	14
Birds of Prey	16
Lizards	18
Snakes	20
Insects and Spiders	22
Frogs and Toads	24
Turtles, Crabs, and Fish	26
Glossary	30
Index	31

2. Chasing
As the zebras run away, she picks out one, and chases it in another direction.

1. Approaching
The lioness approaches a herd of zebras. Other members of her pride wait nearby.

The Big Cats

If you have a pet cat, you know that it is a natural hunter. "Big cats" include lions, tigers, leopards, cheetahs, and jaguars. They are some of the world's fiercest hunters. They often hunt animals larger than themselves.

DID YOU KNOW?

A cheetah can run faster than any other mammal. Its long legs and slender, muscular body help it catch its prey.

3. Catching
The lioness is a swift runner. She soon catches up with and pounces on her victim.

4. Killing and Eating
The other lions join her and they share the meal. The young lions—the cubs—have to wait until the adults have finished.

Fanged Creatures

If you have ever walked into a spider's web, you'll have noticed how sticky it is. Most spiders weave webs to trap flying insects. Some build their webs in holes in the ground. Many spiders, though, are hunters. They go off in search of their prey, which they kill with poisonous fangs. Some spiders hunt during the day. Others strike in the dark.

Amazing!

Many snakes poison their prey, but not the python. Pythons squeeze animals to death by wrapping their long, strong bodies tightly around them. Pythons can kill and swallow very large prey—even a wild pig.

Night Attack
Tarantulas are night hunters. They use their sense of touch to find their victims.

7

Bears

Some bears eat mainly fruits and flowers. Others hunt insects, birds, and larger animals. Polar bears, which live in the icy Arctic regions, are the greatest hunters of all. Like many other bears, they have strong claws and sharp, hooked teeth. They are also good swimmers. They can catch seals, walruses, and even small whales.

Fishing Bears
The world's largest brown bears live in North America. They wade into cold rivers and feed on salmon. They catch the salmon easily, and never have to travel far to find food.

Did You Know?

American black bears eat lots of foods, from nuts and berries to small deer. They live in North American forests. They often climb into trees, where they feed on ants, insects, and honey from bee hives.

A Diving Catch

A polar bear dives into the sea to catch a baby beluga. The bear will kill the whale in the water and then drag it onto the icy surface.

Beware!
Sometimes large sharks attack humans. But it may be only by mistake. Great whites have poor eyesight. As you can see, it would be easy for a shark to mistake a diver, especially one with flippers, for a seal.

Sharks

Sharks are the greatest hunters of the marine world. One of the biggest and most feared of sharks is the great white shark. It has huge jaws and jagged teeth. It feeds on large sea animals such as seals and porpoises. Sharks live in almost all the world's seas. Many sharks are small. These live on small fish and shellfish, which they find on the sandy sea bottom.

DID YOU KNOW?

The largest shark of all is the whale shark. It doesn't have to work hard for its food. It swims around with its huge mouth wide open. Shrimp and other tiny animals flow in and get caught in the shark's gills.

New and Old Teeth
The second row of teeth in this great white's mouth will replace the front teeth when they fall out.

Lazy Hunters

Crocodiles and alligators do not use up a lot of energy. They wait for their food to come to them. One big meal can last them a long time.

Amazing!

American alligators generally feed on fish. They often gather near colonies of water birds, which also eat fish. If it is hungry enough, one of these alligators may even leap suddenly out of the water to snatch a young bird from above the surface.

Scaly Hunters

Like all reptiles, alligators and crocodiles have hard, scaly skin. This helps protect them from attack. They live in and near rivers, lakes, and sea coasts in hot, tropical regions. They are often mistaken for logs

Tooth Troubles
Crocodiles do not chew food. They swallow it in large pieces. However, they often break or lose teeth as they snap their jaws shut. New teeth grow to replace them.

as they float in the water. Depending on their size, they eat different kinds of animals, from small fish to horses—and even people, if the people are careless and get too close.

Whales

Whales live in all the world's oceans. Some kinds live all over the world. Others live only in certain regions. All whales feed on fish and other sea animals. Orcas, or killer whales, are swift and intelligent hunters. They travel in groups and they can often catch and kill whales much bigger than themselves. Their favorite food is seal meat.

Catching Fish on Land
Bottlenose dolphins sometimes help each other hunt. They chase fish toward a river bank or mudflat until they jump out of the water. The dolphins then slide after them and eat them up.

Clever Tactics

Sometimes when seals rest on the beach an orca may swim up to them, causing the frightened seals to jump into the water. This is just what the orcas wanted!

DID YOU KNOW?

The African harrier hawk has a narrow head and long yellow legs, which it uses to pull small animals from their hiding places. This large bird eats young birds, bats, and squirrels.

African harrier hawk

BIRDS OF PREY

Large birds of prey are expert hunters. They have sharp eyesight, which lets them spot their victims from far away. With their wide, powerful wings, they swoop down swiftly and silently. They seize their prey with their strong, sharp talons. Sometimes they carry it off. Sometimes they immediately start to tear at its flesh with their hooked, pointed beaks.

Hunters in the Night
Owls roost in the day and hunt at night. They have large eyes that can see well in dim light. Owls use their strong, curved talons to seize their prey.

Forest Feeder
Huge harpy eagles lurk in South American forests. They often prey on howler monkeys.

Lizards

Most lizards are small. Like other small animals, they are likely to be eaten. Spiders, scorpions, and birds are all out to catch them. Most lizards blend in with their surroundings. This camouflage helps protect them. Some lizards scare enemies away by making themselves look bigger than they really are. Others can roll up and make themselves look smaller.

Amazing!

A red-tailed skink can separate its body from its tail if a bird or other animal is attacking it. The attacker will probably go for the brightly colored tail. The rest of the lizard can then escape. Later, its bright red tail will grow back.

Color Change

The male chameleon can change its camouflage color from dull green to bright red. He is trying to scare other males away.

Stay Away!

This is what the Australian frilled lizard seems to be saying, as it hisses and puffs out the frills of skin at its neck.

SNAKES

All snakes hunt and eat other animals. But snakes are also hunted by other animals, especially birds of prey. Snakes protect themselves from their enemies in different ways. Some make warning noises. Some spit poison. Others disguise themselves by changing color. Hognose snakes and grass snakes are excellent actors. When danger is near, they lie on their back and pretend to be dead. It usually works!

DID YOU KNOW?

Cobras are dangerous snakes. Pipe snakes, which live in Sri Lanka, are not nearly as fierce. But a pipe snake can scare an enemy by pretending to be a cobra. It hides its head and flattens its tail. Then it lifts up the underside of the tail, which looks like a cobra's head.

Attack or Defense?

At the tip of its tail, a rattlesnake has rings that rattle against each other. This snake rattles its tail to frighten its enemies, and sometimes uses it as a mating signal.

Spitting Cobra

Cobras use their poison to kill their prey and to defend themselves. When in danger, they rear up and spit poison through holes in the fronts of their fangs.

INSECTS AND SPIDERS

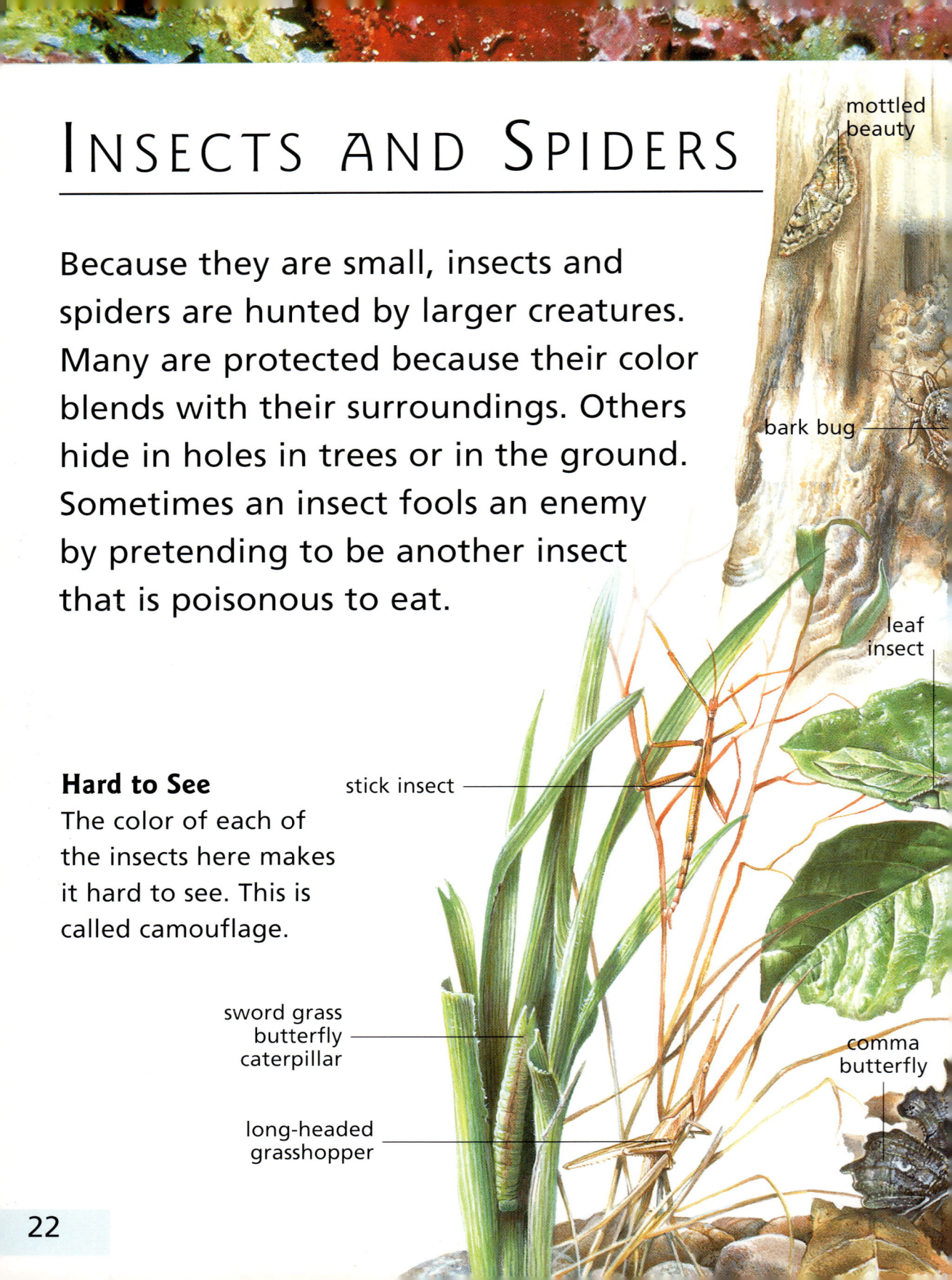

Because they are small, insects and spiders are hunted by larger creatures. Many are protected because their color blends with their surroundings. Others hide in holes in trees or in the ground. Sometimes an insect fools an enemy by pretending to be another insect that is poisonous to eat.

Hard to See
The color of each of the insects here makes it hard to see. This is called camouflage.

mottled beauty

bark bug

leaf insect

stick insect

sword grass butterfly caterpillar

long-headed grasshopper

comma butterfly

22

emerald moth caterpillar

Strange but True

This honeybee did not see the crab spider lurking among the yellow petals. The crab spider is not always yellow. When it moves to another flower, it will slowly turn into the color of that flower's petals.

swallowtail butterfly larva

bush cricket

flower mantis

angle shades moth

cryptic grasshopper

23

Frogs and Toads

If a horned toad sat right in front of you on a rainforest floor, you would probably not notice it. Even sharp-eyed birds of prey perched above might not see it. But while this toad likes to hide, the harlequin frog and the strawberry frog would be hard to miss. Their bright colors are a warning to birds and other predators that they are poisonous.

Harlequin Frog
The poisonous harlequin frog scares predators away with its brightly colored skin.

Poison for Darts

Choco Indians of South America make good use of the poison-dart frog. They rub darts over its skin and then blow the darts through tubes at animals that they eat. The frog's poison quickly kills the animals.

Horned Toad

The horned toad is not only colored like a dead leaf, it is shaped like one, too.

Strawberry Frog

The strawberry frog's skin contains deadly poison.

Safe on the Bottom
A shell covered in algae makes the alligator snapping turtle hard to see.

Turtles, Crabs, and Fish

Just as the house you live in protects you from the wind and weather, turtles' hard shells help to keep them safe. When in danger, they pull themselves

DID YOU KNOW?

Unlike most crabs, the hermit crab does not have a shell. It makes up for it by borrowing one. It lives in shells that sea snails or other sea animals have left behind. From time to time, it finds a new one.

right inside. Often, they are hard to see. Most crabs have hard shells that do the same job as turtles' shells. They are also good at hiding by covering themselves with sponges, algae, or other sea animals.

Spiky Shell
You probably wouldn't pick up a spined turtle with sharp spikes on its shell. Most animals that consider making a meal of it also think twice before grabbing ahold.

Just as a pineapple has spiky skin, the Australian pineapple fish has spikes that protect it. So does the lionfish. The spikes are hidden inside its long fins. Bright colors, too, often spell danger. Any fish that tried to make a meal of the mandarin fish would get a nasty surprise. Its skin has a horrible taste!

Stinger
The lionfish lives on coral reefs. Its 18 hidden spines are sharp and full of poison.

MORE TURTLES, CRABS, AND FISH

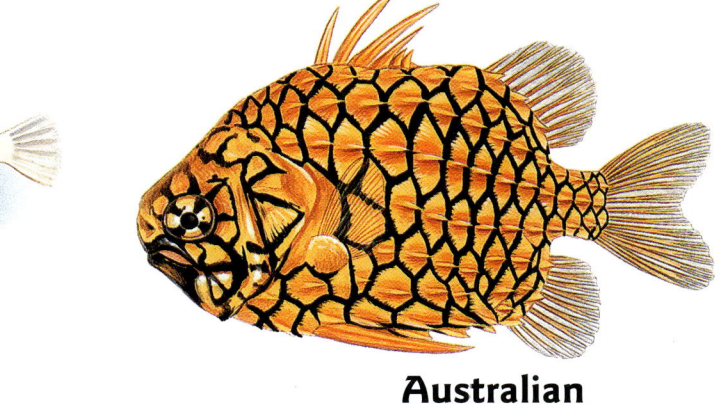

Australian pineapple fish

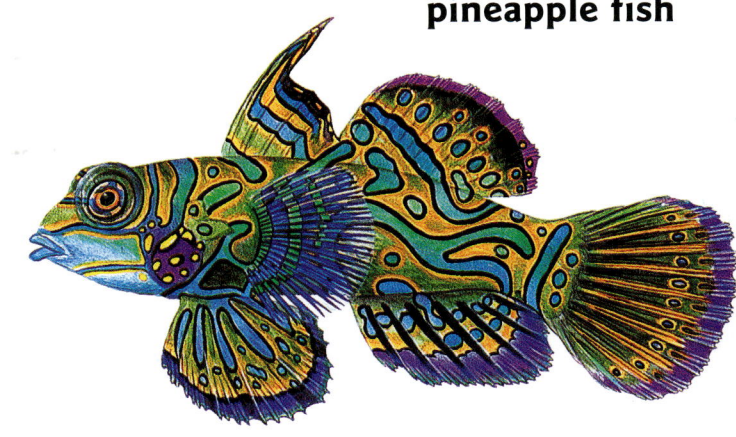

mandarin fish

Fat and Fearsome
When it meets an enemy, a pufferfish starts swallowing water. Soon it swells up and its spines stick out. Now it looks much less tasty than it did before.

DID YOU KNOW?

The mimic filefish (bottom) is not poisonous. But most other fish leave it alone. They mistake it for the black-saddled puffer (top), which *is* poisonous. Can you spot the differences?

29

Glossary

algae Simple water plants that have no stems or flowers. Seaweeds are algae.

beluga A white whale that lives in cold Arctic seas.

bird of prey A bird that hunts other birds and animals and eats their flesh.

chameleon A small lizard that can change its color to blend in with its surroundings.

fangs Long, sharp teeth that spiders and snakes use to inject poison into their prey.

mammal An animal that grows inside its mother's body before it is born. The young drink their mother's milk.

prey Animals that are caught and eaten by other animals.

reptile A cold-blooded animal that has a backbone and dry skin covered by scales or a hard shell.

spines Sharp spikes that stick out from the body of some types of fish and other animals, such as porcupines.

talons Sharp, curved claws that birds of prey have on their feet.

Index

alligators	12
bears	8–9
birds	8, 12, 16–17, 20, 24
camouflage	18, 19, 22–23
cheetahs	4, 5
crabs	26–27
crocodiles	12, 13
fish	10, 12, 13, 14, 28, 29
frogs	24–25
insects	6, 8, 22–23
lions	4–5
lizards	18–19
sharks	10–11
snakes	6, 20–21
spiders	6–7, 18, 22–23
toads	24–25
turtles	26–27
whales	8, 9, 14–15

Picture and Illustration Credits

[t=top, b=bottom, l=left, r=right, c=center, F=front, B=back, C=cover, bg=background]

Corel Corporation 5cl, 8tr, 8br, 11tr, 13tr, 12cl, 14 bl, 17tr, 21tr, 30b, 18–32 borders. **Christer Eriksson** 6–7c, 9c, 10–11c, 14–15c, 16–17c, 18–19c, 26c, FC. **Ray Grinaway** 23tl. **Robert Hynes** 19tl, 22–23c, 31tl. **David Kirshner** 1c, 2b, 3t, 6b, 12–13c, 18bl, 20br, 21c, 21tl, 24bl, 24–25bc, 25rc, 25tr, 27bl, 29tr, 29rc, 29bl. **Frank Knight** 4–5c, 27tl, 29tl. **Photodisc** 4–17 borders, Cbg. **Tony Pyrzakowski** 16tl. **Bernard Tate** 28c.

Books in This Series

WEIRD AND WONDERFUL WILDLIFE	LAND, SEA, AND SKY	INFORMATION STATION
Incredible Creatures	Sharks and Rays	Every Body Tells a Story
Creepy Creatures	Underwater Animals	The Human Body
Scaly Things	Mammals of the Sea	Bright Ideas
Feathers and Flight	Ocean Life	Out and About
Attack and Defense	Volcanoes	Exploring Space
Snakes	Weather Watching	High Flying
Hidden World	Maps and Our World	How Things Work
Reptiles and Amphibians	Earthquakes	Native Americans
Mini Mammals	The Plant Kingdom	Travelers and Traders
Up and Away	Rain or Shine	Sports for All
Mighty Mammals	Sky Watch	People from the Past
Dangerous Animals	The Planets	Play Ball!

Murphy School
Woodridge School Dist. 68
Woodridge, IL 60517